SUPERWOMEN ROLE MODELS

RUTH BADER GINSBURG

Heather Moore Niver

PowerKiDS press™

New York

Published in 2017 by The Rosen Publishing Group, Inc.
29 East 21st Street, New York, NY 10010

First Edition

Editor: Katie Kawa
Book Design: Reann Nye

Photo Credits: Cover, pp. 1–32 (halftone pattern) Solomin Andrey/Shutterstock.com; cover, p. 1 http://commons.wikimedia.org/wiki/File:Ruth_Bader_Ginsburg_official_SCOTUS_portrait.jpg; p. 5 Stringer/Hulton Archive/Getty Images; p. 7 Terry Ashe/The LIFE Images Collection/Getty Images; p. 9 Karin Cooper/Hulton Archive/Getty Images; p. 11 https://commons.wikimedia.org/wiki/File:Harvard_Law_School_Library_in_Langdell_Hall_at_night.jpg; p. 13 Rob Crandall/Shutterstock.com; p. 15 https://commons.wikimedia.org/wiki/File:O%27Connor,_Sotomayor,_Ginsburg,_and_Kagan.jpg; p. 17 The Washington Post/Getty Images; p. 19 SAUL LOEB/AP Images; p. 21 Justin Sullivan/Getty Images News/Getty Images; p. 23 Alex Wong/Getty Images News/Getty Images; p. 25 Allison Shelley/Getty Images News/Getty Images; p. 27 Pool/Getty Images News/Getty Images; p. 29 Bill Clark/Bloomberg/Getty Images; p. 30 Bloomberg/Getty Images.

Library of Congress Cataloging-in-Publication Data

Names: Niver, Heather Moore, author.
Title: Ruth Bader Ginsburg / Heather Moore Niver.
Description: New York : PowerKids Press, 2016. | Series: Superwomen role
  models | Includes index.
Identifiers: LCCN 2015044021 | ISBN 9781508148272 (pbk.) | ISBN 9781508147787 (6 pack) |
ISBN 9781508148135 (library bound)
Subjects: LCSH: Ginsburg, Ruth Bader–Juvenile literature. | Judges–United
  States–Biography–Juvenile literature. | Women judges–United
  States–Biography–Juvenile literature. | United States. Supreme
  Court–Biography–Juvenile literature.
Classification: LCC KF8745.G56 N58 2016 | DDC 347.73/2634–dc23
LC record available at http://lccn.loc.gov/2015044021

Manufactured in the United States of America

CPSIA Compliance Information: Batch #BS16PK: For Further Information contact Rosen Publishing, New York, New York at 1-800-237-9932

CONTENTS

NOTORIOUS R.B.G.

Ruth Bader Ginsburg may be small in **stature**, but the role she's played in the fight for equality for all Americans is anything but small. How did this Supreme Court justice get the nickname "The Notorious R.B.G," which is a play on the name of the famously large and tough rapper The Notorious B.I.G.? Ruth has fiercely fought for equality, especially women's rights. Her thoughts and opinions are strong, whether she's in court or in public. She's definitely a force to be reckoned with.

Ruth was the second woman to be named a justice of the United States Supreme Court, after Sandra Day O'Connor. Ruth is currently the oldest justice on the bench, but she's far from finished with her work toward equality for all!

Ruth Bader Ginsburg has gained fame and earned respect for her strong opinions and the way she fights for what she believes in.

NOT AN EASY CHILDHOOD

On March 15, 1933, Ruth Joan Bader was born to Nathan and Celia Bader. Ruth was raised in Brooklyn, New York, during the Great Depression, which was a period of worldwide economic hardship and unemployment. Ruth's father worked as a **furrier**. Unfortunately, not many people bought furs during the Great Depression. It was a tough time for people, including the Baders. Ruth had a sister, Marilyn, but she died when Ruth was still young.

Celia Bader taught her daughters how important it was to get a good education. Ruth's mother didn't go to college. She worked in a factory making clothes in order to pay for her brother to go to college. Celia also taught her daughters to be independent women who could think for themselves.

IN HER WORDS

"My mother told me two things constantly. One was to be a lady, and the other was to be independent. The study of law was unusual for women of my generation. For most girls growing up in the '40s, the most important degree was not your B.A. [college degree], but your M.R.S. [married name]."

Interview for the American Civil Liberties Union's (ACLU's) "Tribute: The Legacy of Ruth Bader Ginsburg and WRP Staff"

Ruth grew up during a difficult time in American history. Her parents—especially her mother—taught her how important it was to be strong and smart.

SCHOOL DAYS

Celia never got to see her daughter go to college. She died of cancer the day before Ruth graduated from James Madison High School. Ruth then attended Cornell University in Ithaca, New York, where she met another law student named Martin Ginsburg, who was often called Marty. They married in 1954, shortly after Ruth graduated at the very top of her class. Later that year, Marty was called up to join the military, and Ruth gave birth to their first child, Jane.

By 1956, Marty was discharged, or let out of the military. They moved their little family to Massachusetts, where they both enrolled as students at Harvard Law School. Ruth was one of only nine women in her law school class. The school's dean criticized women for taking spots he believed should have gone to men.

IN HER WORDS

"Neither of my parents had the means to attend college, but both taught me to love learning, to care about people, and to work hard for whatever I wanted or believed in."
Statement from the U.S. Senate hearings concerning Ruth's nomination to the U.S. Supreme Court, given in July 1993

Ruth and Marty were married for 56 years. Marty died of cancer in 2010.

NEW CHALLENGES

Ruth didn't give up in the face of harsh attitudes toward women. Instead, she went on to excel in all her classes. She also became the famous Harvard Law Review's first female member. During all this, Ruth continued to take care of her family, too.

Marty was **diagnosed** with cancer while he and Ruth were at Harvard. He had to undergo serious treatment, and he was slow to heal. Not only did Ruth tend to her husband's needs while he was sick and recovering, she went to his classes, took notes for him, and helped type his papers! Marty eventually recovered and graduated. The family then moved to New York City, where he worked at a law firm. Ruth chose to continue her studies in New York City.

A STRONG MARRIAGE

Marty and Ruth had a strong and supportive marriage. He was very outgoing, while she's more reserved. Marty was also a great cook, while Ruth is rarely in the kitchen. They had two children: Jane and a son named James. Ruth now has four grandchildren. Before Marty died in 2010, he left a note for Ruth in which he told her, "...I have admired and loved you almost since the day we first met at Cornell some 56 years ago."

Ruth was the first woman to be a part of the Harvard Law Review. This organization, which publishes a law journal, is made up of some of the brightest students at Harvard Law School, shown here.

NEW YORK

When Ruth and her young family moved to New York City, she transferred to Columbia Law School. At Columbia, she was again selected for the school's law review, and she graduated first in her class in 1959. Even though Ruth excelled at just about everything she did, she still faced gender **discrimination** as she started to look for work after graduation.

Ruth worked as a law clerk for a judge named Edmund L. Palmieri from 1959 to 1961. In 1963, Ruth began working as a law professor at Rutgers University in New Jersey. She remained there until 1972, when she transferred to work at her **alma mater**, Columbia. Ruth became the first **tenured** female professor in Columbia's history. Ruth worked there until 1980.

WOMEN'S RIGHTS AND EQUALITY

In 1972, Ruth helped found the Women's Rights Project for the ACLU. Ruth became known as a leading lawyer in the women's rights movement. Six of the cases she argued before the Supreme Court focused on gender discrimination. These are now considered **landmark cases**. Ruth defended both men and women. She argued that gender discrimination is bad for people of both genders.

Ruth won five of the six landmark gender discrimination cases she argued. Women's rights and equality for all have continued to be important to Ruth throughout her legal career.

REACHING THE SUPREME COURT

In 1980, President Jimmy Carter nominated Ruth to the United States Court of Appeals for the District of Columbia Circuit. On June 30, 1980, she was sworn in, and Marty moved with her to Washington, D.C. Before long, Ruth became known as a **centrist**. She tried not to interpret the law through one set of political views. Ruth was the kind of independent thinker her mother wanted her to become.

In 1993, President Bill Clinton needed to fill a spot on the Supreme Court after Byron R. White stepped down. He nominated Ruth as associate justice of the Supreme Court to fill White's seat. On August 10, 1993, she was sworn in as a justice of the highest court in the United States.

THE CAMPAIGN

During the months President Clinton spent deciding who to nominate for White's empty Supreme Court spot, the Ginsburgs were busy making sure he noticed Ruth. Marty even organized letter-writing campaigns! A president can't just pick a candidate for the Supreme Court and make it instantly official. The nomination has to be approved by the Senate after a series of hearings. The U.S. Senate approved Ruth 96 to 3!

SANDRA DAY O'CONNOR

SONIA SOTOMAYOR

RUTH BADER GINSBURG

ELENA KAGAN

When Ruth was sworn in to the U.S. Supreme Court, she and Sandra Day O'Connor were the only female justices. As of 2015, there are three women serving on the Supreme Court: Ruth, Elena Kagan, and Sonia Sotomayor.

Once Ruth took her place among her fellow Supreme Court justices in 1993, she quickly earned a reputation for working hard and being unafraid to ask questions. She was often the first to ask questions of lawyers arguing their cases before the Supreme Court. Now, over 20 years after she first became a Supreme Court justice, she's still known for her quick questions.

Ruth is also known for the opinions she's written. An opinion is a written explanation for a legal decision. Ruth has written both majority opinions, which state how the court officially ruled on an issue, and dissents, which are opinions that go against the majority decision of the court. People respect Ruth for the level-headed reasoning she's used throughout her career, especially in her written opinions.

IN HER WORDS

"I try to teach through my opinions, through my speeches, how wrong it is to judge people on the basis of what they look like, color of their skin, whether they're men or women."
Interview with Irin Carmon of MSNBC's The Rachel Maddow Show, which aired on February 16, 2015

Ruth earned the respect of her fellow Supreme Court justices by asking intelligent questions more quickly than any other justice.

CONTINUING THE FIGHT

During her time on the Supreme Court, Ruth has continued to fight for women's rights. In 1996, she wrote the majority opinion in the case of *United States v. Virginia*. This was a landmark case concerning education for women in the United States. The Virginia Military Institute had a male-only admissions policy, which meant women couldn't go to school there. The Supreme Court ruled 7 to 1 that this policy was unconstitutional, so the school couldn't refuse to admit women any longer.

Ruth was also a vocal supporter of the Lilly Ledbetter Fair Pay Act, which became a law when it was signed by President Barack Obama in 2009. This act makes it easier for women to fight in court for equal pay for equal work.

IN HER WORDS

"…when I'm sometimes asked, 'When will there be enough [women on the Supreme Court]?,' and I say, 'When there are nine,' people are shocked. But there'd been nine men, and nobody's ever raised a question about that."

Remarks given during the 10th Circuit Bench & Bar Conference at the University of Colorado in October 2012

The Lilly Ledbetter Fair Pay Act was the first piece of legislation Barack Obama signed as president. He gave a copy of the signed act to Ruth to thank her for fighting for equality as strongly as she has throughout her career.

MARRIAGE EQUALITY

On June 26, 2015, the Supreme Court ruled on the landmark case of *Obergefell v. Hodges*. In a 5 to 4 decision, the court ruled that same-sex marriage should be made legal throughout the United States. Ruth was part of the majority, along with Justices Anthony Kennedy, Stephen Breyer, Sonia Sotomayor, and Elena Kagan.

Ruth had been an active and visible supporter of marriage equality for years before the *Obergefell v. Hodges* ruling. In 2013, she **presided** over the wedding of economist John Roberts and Michael Kaiser, who, at that time, was the president of the John F. Kennedy Center for the Performing Arts. Ruth is believed to be the first Supreme Court justice to preside over a same-sex marriage ceremony.

Equality has always been important to Ruth. She's known as a champion of both women's rights and marriage equality, which has made her very popular with many young Americans.

RIVALS!

Most of the time, Justices Stephen Breyer, Sonia Sotomayor, and Elena Kagan are in Ruth's corner. This group usually agrees about how to interpret the U.S. Constitution. The same couldn't be said of Ruth and Justice Antonin Scalia, who died in February 2016. The Scalia-Ginsburg rivalry was infamous! They often disagreed and had lively debates.

Off the bench, however, the two were good friends for years. "If you can't disagree **ardently** with your **colleagues** about some issue of the law and yet personally still be friends, get another job, for Pete's sake," Antonin once said. He and Ruth often took vacations together, and they spent New Year's Eve together every year. They liked and respected each other as people, even though they had different opinions about the law and the U.S. Constitution.

INSPIRING AN OPERA

Ruth and Antonin had similar interests outside of work. What really brought them together was their love of opera, so it seems fitting that composer Derrick Wang was reading through their dissents and was inspired by their drama. He wrote to the two justices to ask for their approval to write the opera *Scalia/Ginsburg*. They both gave their approval, and the opera had its world premiere in July 2015.

Ruth and Antonin proved that you don't always have to agree with your friends about everything to enjoy their company.

HER OWN STYLE

Ruth has many interests beyond the law. She enjoys traveling. Ruth also loves going to the opera. She's been spotted at opera performances everywhere from New York to New Mexico. In fact, she's spent many summers in Santa Fe, New Mexico, because she's such a big fan of their opera company.

Besides having a sharp mind and an ear for opera music, Ruth has a flair for eye-catching fashion. When she's not on the bench, she often wears bright, interesting clothes from around the world. Ruth is also known for wearing long gloves or shorter lace gloves. Even when she's on the bench, she might wear a lace collar over her black robe. She's also been known to wear big earrings to make a bold fashion statement.

Ruth started wearing gloves while being treated for **colon** cancer in 1999. They helped protect her from germs that could make her sicker. Now, she wears them because she likes the way they look.

SMALL BUT MIGHTY

Ruth is just over 5 feet (1.5 m) tall. She moves slowly, eats slowly, and speaks with so many pauses that listeners aren't sure if she will continue. However, she's also known as a very strong woman. Not even cancer could stop her from working.

In 1999, Ruth went through treatment for colon cancer, and in 2009, she was diagnosed with **pancreatic** cancer. In both cases, Ruth never missed a day on the bench. She had heart surgery in 2014, but she quickly returned to work after that, too.

Fitness is important to Ruth. She exercises often and even got a personal trainer after her battle with colon cancer. Ruth wants to keep working, and she knows she has to keep her body fit and healthy in order to do that.

Although Ruth looks small, she's tough—both in court and in the gym!

WHAT SHE DOESN'T PLAN TO DO

Many people ask Ruth when she might be ready to retire. However, as of 2016, Ruth has no such plans! She believes in taking things one year at a time. She may be the oldest justice on the Supreme Court, but she doesn't believe she's ready to retire yet, and many people agree with her.

In fact, Ruth might be more popular now than ever before. She inspires young people today—especially young women—to fight for equal rights for all people. Ruth is the subject of many books, she's mentioned on many television shows, and there's even a popular **Tumblr** page dedicated to "The Notorious R.B.G."

Ruth worked hard to find success and has used that success to fight for equality. She's a true superwoman role model!

IN HER WORDS

"[I want to be remembered as] someone who used whatever talent she had to do her work to the very best of her ability. And to help repair tears in her society, to make things a little better through the use of whatever ability she has. To do something, as my colleague David Souter would say, outside myself. [Because] I've gotten much more satisfaction for the things that I've done for which I was not paid."
Interview with Irin Carmon of MSNBC's *The Rachel Maddow Show*, **which aired on February 16, 2015**

Ruth has said, "At my advanced age…I'm constantly amazed by the number of people who want to take my picture." At 83 years old, she continues to inspire young people to dream big, work hard, and help others.

TIMELINE

March 15, 1933: Ruth Jane Bader is born in Brooklyn, New York.

June 23, 1954: Ruth marries Martin (Marty) Ginsburg.

1956: Ruth and Marty begin studying at Harvard Law School.

1959: Ruth graduates from Columbia Law School.

1963: Ruth begins teaching at Rutgers University School of Law.

1972: Ruth begins teaching at Columbia University and co-founds the Women's Rights Project for the ACLU.

1980: President Jimmy Carter nominates Ruth as a judge of the U.S. Court of Appeals for the District of Columbia Circuit.

1993: President Bill Clinton nominates Ruth for the United States Supreme Court.

1996: Ruth writes the majority opinion in the landmark case of *United States v. Virginia*.

June 26, 2015: Ruth votes in favor of making same-sex marriage legal throughout the United States in the case of *Obergefell v. Hodges*.

GLOSSARY

alma mater: A school from which someone graduated.

ardently: Done with strong feelings.

centrist: A person who holds moderate political views.

colleague: A fellow worker at the same job.

colon: A part of the large intestine.

diagnose: To identify a disease by its signs and symptoms.

discrimination: Different—usually unfair—treatment based on factors such as a person's race, age, religion, or gender.

furrier: A person who sells furs.

landmark case: A court case that is important because it sets a new legal precedent, or example.

pancreatic: Relating to the pancreas, a body part near the stomach that produces substances to help the body use and break down food.

preside: To be in a position of authority at a meeting, gathering, or ceremony.

stature: A person's natural height.

tenure: A guarantee of employment, especially for a teacher.

Tumblr: A website that allows users to post microblogs, or short, frequent pieces of content.

INDEX

WEBSITES

Due to the changing nature of Internet links, PowerKids Press has developed an online list of websites related to the subject of this book. This site is updated regularly. Please use this link to access the list: www.powerkidslinks.com/sprwmn/rbg